Alison Joh

UNDERSTANDING
Y O U R V A L U E I S
PRICELESS

Forty days of inspiring God-anointed words to enrich
your life and guide you on your spiritual journey.

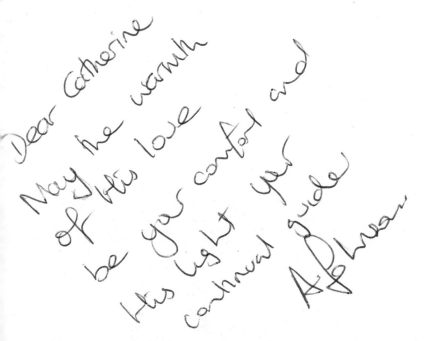

Dear Catherine
May the warmth
of His love
be your comfort and
His light your
continual guide
A Phelan

First published 2012 by Fast-Print Publishing of Peterborough, England.

www.fast-print.net/store.php

UNDERSTANDING YOUR VALUE IS PRICELESS
Copyright © Alison Johnson 2012

ISBN: 978-178035-492-7

A catalogue record for this book is available from the British Library

An environmentally friendly book printed and bound in England by
www.printondemand-worldwide.com

This book is made entirely of chain-of-custody materials

Acknowledgements

Thank you to Pastor Martin and Pastor Sandy Phelps for believing in me and entrusting me with the privilege of heading up the women's ministry at Rhema Church London. Your passionate following of Christ and your desire to walk out His vision for the church never ceases to amaze me. Your belief that the Rhema congregation should receive word-based teaching is what will see it continue to grow from strength to strength. You relentlessly pursue God and His plans and press on when others would have faltered. I have been blessed from the moment I entered the doors.

Thank you to Sherise Hobbs for proofreading the drafts at different stages and for being so patient and encouraging. It is much appreciated.

Thank you to all the women who have attended the Rhema Leading Ladies workshops and been open to the word of God and for sharing your testimonies as well. To everyone who has prayed this into being I thank you. The work has just begun so we must remain vigilant and committed to prayer.

Last, but not at all least, a huge thank you to my wonderful family who have given me the time and support and just allowed me the space to get this book written. Much love always to you.

Introduction

I am a wife, mother of four daughters, grandmother to one, women's minister, social entrepreneur, motivational speaker, trainer and philanthropist. As a woman (first and foremost) and a mother of four precious and beautiful girls my heart always beats for the emotional well-being of females.

It is a thread that has always existed in my work, even to spreading my wings and setting up my own company. I have heard countless stories of females of all ages who have suffered much, lost their self respect, had their esteem trampled on and fought to really understand just who they are.

As a passionate Christian I know that the essence of a female's identity is contained in the truth of the gospel. When a female understands who her spiritual Father is she is able to grow in confidence and accept her rightful position as a princess who is destined to be Queen. She will know that she is part of a chosen race who has been born to fulfil a great purpose within God's plan.

The affirmations are designed for you to read out loud and have them as your daily confession. There is power in the words that we speak and our lives are formed by our words. So therefore make a promise to yourself that you will speak words of life and not death over your life and any situation you may find yourself in.

Don't be discouraged if you miss a day. This book can be read in many ways and at any time of day. Once you get to Day Forty, you may decide to flip straight back to Day One and start all over again!

My prayer for every female who reads this is that you get the revelation of your true value and allow your identity to be formed and moulded by God. When you understand your value you will understand that you are priceless.

Love

AJ

'But if we walk in the light as He is in the light, we have fellowship with one another , and the blood of Jesus Christ His son cleanses us from all sin' (John 1:7, NKJV)

'I will seek what was lost and bring back what was driven away, bind up the broken and strengthen what was sick'

Ezekiel 34:16 (NKJV)

You have always been on God's mind. He is the Father that will go looking for the one who needs Him. Just like a shepherd would go searching for one lost sheep so too will our Father in heaven come searching for you. Even if you have been rejected and pushed away by others He wants you because He loves you eternally. He will bind up your broken-ness and strengthen the places where people and situations have caused you to be weakened.

You are His daughter and He will repair, rebuild and restore you.

Affirmation: I will seek you Lord all the days of my life.

Day 2:

'The Lord is the strength of my life; of whom shall I be afraid?'

Psalm 27:1 (NKJV)

Sometimes in life we are faced with challenges that seem insurmountable. There are situations that arise that seem to sap our energy and make us feel weak. People may turn against you and even cause you to become frightened. Quite sadly these are the times we are living in. But I want you to know that when you serve an almighty, powerful, miracle-working God who is alive and sits on the throne then you do not have to be afraid. He is your strength, so lean on Him with confidence. There is no-one you have to fear for He has covered you.

Faith conquers fear and enables you to embrace the journey into righteousness.

Affirmation: I place my fears on the altar. I am free.

Day 3:

'The liberal person shall be enriched, and he who waters shall himself be watered'

Proverbs 11:25 (NKJV)

A scarcity mindset operates in fear and believes that there is not enough to go around. A giving mindset operates in faith and knows that there is more than enough for everyone. There are many who have more than enough and yet never give anyone anything. The word tells us that the person who gives freely will also be blessed in return. You cannot feed the hungry and be without food; you cannot house others and be homeless; you cannot clothe the naked and be without clothes yourself.

A lawyer asked Jesus, 'Who is my neighbour?' The answer is anyone that needs help, and everyone needs help at some point in their life. Determine today to help your neighbour and experience the fulfilment of blessing others.

Affirmation: I will seek new ways to bless others.

'For her worth is far above rubies'

Proverbs 31:10 (NKJV)

1. They are extremely strong
2. All rubies have flaws and yet are more valuable in terms of price than that of diamonds
3. Rubies have been found all over the world
4. Symbolism of rubies – devotion, integrity, courage and happiness

The word tells us that we are MORE precious than the most expensive gem known to mankind. This is an essential truth that you need to get a revelation of. When you understand your value you will speak and act in a different manner. You will not 'sell' yourself short or cheaply. God has created you as a special, beautiful and valued member of his family. God lovingly knit our bones together in our mother's womb and created us to be unique. Out of the 7bn people in this world there is no-one like you.

Affirmation: I am a key person of influence (KPI) - Important and valuable.

Day 5:

'Your fame went out among the nations because of your beauty, for it was perfect through My splendour which I had bestowed on you, says the Lord God'

Ezekiel 16:14 (NKJV)

In The Message version of the Bible it states that 'you were absolutely stunning'. The gospel holds the truth and no wonder it is referred to as the good news because we were created beautiful and named as such by God our heavenly Father.

Don't allow the comments of others to eat away at your self esteem. Don't let doubt creep in about how you look. Declare with absolute confidence that you are a child of a living God who named you after himself. You carry His splendour upon you.

Affirmation: I am beautiful because He created me that way.

Day 6:

'I pray that the eyes of your heart may be enlightened, so that you will know what is the hope of His calling, what are the riches of the glory of His inheritance in the saints'

Ephesians 1:18 (NKJV)

God has an intention for you. He has an aim and a purpose for you. Trust in Him and draw close. Speak to Him through prayer like you would communicate with a trusted, loyal friend. Ask God what the hope of his calling is for you.

Some of your plans may not have worked out so far but God has bigger and better things planned for you. Often the situations we have overcome hold clues as to the direction and the people that God may want us to follow and minister to.

Affirmation: I believe in God's plan for my life.

Day 7:

'But the Lord replied to her by saying, "Martha, Martha you are anxious and troubled about many things. There is need of only one or but a few things. Mary has chosen the good portion which shall not be taken away from her"

Luke 10:41 (NKJV)

It is so easy to get pulled in many directions by the often conflicting demands on our lives. We rush around attempting to complete as many things as possible. I'm sure many of you could be crowned multi-tasker of the decade! But we need to be mindful tthat in all the rushing and in all the work we don't lose sight of what is really important.

Martha busied herself with household chores when Jesus visited but Mary sat quietly at his feet. The word tells us that Mary chose the good portion. Set aside time to pray, read your bible and communicate with Him.

Affirmation: I will focus my eyes on you and understand my true priorities.

'For I (myself) will give you a mouth and such utterance and wisdom that all of your foes combined will be unable to stand against or refute'

Luke 21:15 (NKJV)

It is a well-documented fact that women speak faster than men and also use a lot more words in any given day. Our mouths can in fact act as weapons, able to slice and dice people as fast as we can blink. However, when we learn to rely on God and seek Him in our seasons of injustice, irritation, anger and frustration He will fill our mouths with Godly wisdom.

Godly wisdom has a power that our own words do not contain. The brightest intellectual could prepare an argument and God can provide you with words to confound and confuse their debate. Allow Him to take control of your mouth and your words and watch out for the transformation in your circumstances.

Affirmation: Dear Father, fill my mouth with your words so I may speak on things in a way that is pleasing to you.

Day 9:

'The Lord God has given me the tongue of the learned. That I should know how to speak a word in season to him who is weary'

Isaiah 50:4 (NKJV)

Sometimes you have to follow the quiet voice that urges you to step out and be bold. You may not usually be the kind of person that can approach another. You may feel shy, unsure of yourself or your abilities to help. God will guide you and show you who to approach and give you ways of helping them. Even if you look at your natural circumstances – for example, exam results, qualifications, status of employment etc etc and determine that you are not fit or able to help. Let me tell you that those are the world's criteria and not God's.

He has qualified you to speak a word at the right time and in the right place to the person who needs your particular kind of help.

Affirmation: Thank you Father for you have called me able and I am qualified because of you.

Day 10:

'A time to weep and a time to laugh, a time to mourn and a time to dance'

Ecclesiastes 3:4 (NKJV)

There is a time to weep. There will be situations that will cause tears and unhappiness. But the good news is there will also be a time to laugh. We have to understand that it is not our portion to remain in the place of weeping and mourning. The promise is that there will be different seasons. We have to almost give ourselves permission to move from one state to another. We have to recognise that seasons end and new ones begin.

When I lost a dear childhood friend in 1995 I felt like I would never smile again and yet months later when I gave birth to my third daughter I praised God and felt my joy return.

Affirmation: The world did not give me my joy so therefore it cannot take it away

'Then the woman of Samaria said to Him, "How is it that You, being a Jew, ask a drink from me, a Samaritan woman?" For Jews have no dealings with Samaritans'

John 4:9 (NKJV)

Have you ever been in a situation where you have questioned your worthiness?

What we need to get a revelation of is that we are not 'patched-up sinners' but born-again Christians with renewed thinking and fresh understanding. God has created us to be part of his royal household. When we get a hold of who we really are as one of God's daughters we can be confident and our self esteem will be raised. Your gender, ethnicity, cultural background, age, size, financial position, where you live, who you work for and your marital status have no bearing whatsoever.

When you make the decision that God is the centre of your worthiness you can hold your head up high. You can believe and walk in the authority that has been placed within you. You are worthy, beautiful and have immense value.

Affirmation: I have been fearfully and wonderfully made.

Day 12:

'A gracious woman retains honour'

Proverbs 11:16 (NKJV)

When we believe that we have been created as gracious women, ones who are the children of the Lord God, then we know we have the ability to be honourable in all situations. There are many situations that can arise, for example - conflict, lies, betrayal, misunderstandings, temptation, disagreement and challenge, but we have a choice as to how we behave in each scenario. Despite what difficulties or temptations we may encounter we can choose to retain honour and walk in integrity. This means in turn that we set good examples to those around us by allowing God to shine from within.

My sister, being gracious isn't always the easy option but it is the way that leads to blessings and fulfilment.

Affirmation: I will honour God with my words and my actions.

Day 13:

'He didn't go off and leave us, He didn't abandon us defenceless'

Psalm 124:6-8 (The Message)

There are people that you have relied on who have let you down. They have made promises they chose not to keep, been fickle and even in some cases betrayed and abandoned you. It is easy in those scenarios to feel scared, angry, confused and often become bitter. You may have been abandoned and betrayed but the Word assures us that God will never do that. Even when Jesus left this earth He left us with His Holy Spirit to live within us so we would never be alone.

If you haven't already, you can make the choice to be part of God's family and to take your rightful place as one of His daughters.

My sister, you are not alone or abandoned by Him. When others may be fickle, changeable, unreliable and untrustworthy God is a solid rock on whom you can always rely.

Affirmation: I am not alone and I place my trust in Him.

Day 14:

'Who has saved us and called us with a holy calling, not according to our works, but according to His own purpose and grace which was given to us in Christ Jesus before time began'

Timothy 1:9 (NKJV)

It is not about how much we can do for God that will get us into His favour. The word tells us that it is not according to our works but that God has called us according to the purpose He has in mind for us. His grace is sufficient to cover us in every situation and we need to get hold of the revelation that His plan existed before we did. We need to understand that we are part of a royal priesthood and have inherited the promises of our ancestors in the Bible.

'You' have a holy calling! Start celebrating today!

Affirmation: Heavenly Father, I believe in your plan for me.

Day 15:

'Take heed to yourselves, lest your heart be deceived, and you turn aside and serve other gods and worship them'

Deuteronomy 11:16 (NKJV)

Facebook, Ebay, handbags, shoes, TV programmes, make-up and magazines. I bet you're smiling to yourself because you know just how much time and money you spend on these things. I'm sure that when you first read the scripture at the top you thought, 'I don't serve other gods', but in actual fact there is a chance you may do! Serving other gods comes in many forms. We can see from the list above that we can easily become obsessed by material things which take us away from the time and energy that we could invest in our relationship with God. When these things take more and more of our time then we are in danger of 'worshipping' them.

When was the last time you spent even 10 minutes in every day reading the Word or even praying? Let us be diligent in our worship.

Affirmation: I will make time for the things of God and build my relationship with Him day by day.

'The angel said to her "Rejoice, highly favoured one, the Lord is with you, blessed are you among women'

Luke 1:28 (NKJV)

When the angel of the Lord visited Mary he called her 'blessed among women' Mary laughed at first feeling sure that he had addressed her incorrectly. The name that God (or indeed His messengers) will give us as they greet us may sound strange to your ears. How we see ourselves and how God sees us is usually in two different ways.

There is a gap between our understanding and confidence in who we are and who He knows He created. We are blessed and favoured among women because we have accepted the Lord Jesus Christ as our Lord and saviour. Just as Mary ultimately said – 'May it be according to your word' – then let us too confess the same.

Affirmation: I am blessed in abundance and will walk and talk as a daughter of the king.

'There is laid up for me the crown of righteousness, which the Lord, the righteous Judge, will give to me on that day...'

2 Timothy 4:8 (NKJV)

Put aside any thoughts of you being ordinary and not of any real value. Today fill yourself afresh with renewed hope and excitement. The Word tells us that God has already set aside the crown of righteousness for us. We are going to reach that day because He has declared that we will. The world may judge you, condemn you and undervalue you but God does not. He knows your name and who you are. This promise is just one of over 7,000 in the Bible. Take hold of this today and every day that passes because you are His daughter and your Father has made this promise to you.

Affirmation: My focus is on what lies ahead. God has promised me my crown of righteousness.

Day 18:

'You are the light of the world. A city that is set on a hill cannot be hidden. Nor do they light a lamp and put it under a basket, but on a lampstand, and it gives light to all who are in the house. Let your light so shine before men, that they may see your good works and glorify your Father in heaven'

Matthew 5:14-16 (NKJV)

There is a slogan I saw recently that was promoting the energy industry. It read, 'Where there is light, there is power'. We are the light of the world, ladies, so it follows that we have power. God who lives within us gives us energy and power to overcome all things. Even when we feel weak the word assures us that in our weakness then His perfect strength shall be revealed.

'You are the light of the world' – this is a bold statement. When you commit your life to Christ you receive this as your inheritance. You don't have to hide your talents, skills and abilities. You bless the world by displaying your light and in turn this brings glory to God. There are those who will be witnessed to by your transformation and they may come to know Christ only because of you.

Remember simple acts of kindness speak volumes and they help to shed God's light wherever we are.

Affirmation: My light has been given to me by my Heavenly Father and I am going to let it shine.

'But Hannah answered, "No, my lord, I am a woman of a sorrowful spirit. I have drunk neither wine nor strong drink, but I was pouring out my soul before the Lord'

1 Samuel 1:15 (NKJV)

Hannah is observed by Eli the priest whilst she is praying in the temple. He sees her mouth moving and yet no sound was heard. Eli then believes that Hannah must be drunk. The reality was Hannah was talking to God from her very soul. Hannah was making her entreaty to God in respect of her not having any children. This was a deeply personal issue and one which was causing her much distress. There are times in our lives when the matter or issue is so personal to us that words cannot fully describe what it is we are requesting. There is a place deep inside us that is able to speak to God and communicate our innermost thoughts and feelings.

Hannah tells Eli 'I was pouring out my soul'. Others observing you may not understand why you are praying in this manner but that doesn't matter because you know the petition you are making and most importantly God is in position to not only hear you but also respond.

Affirmation: I will place all my sorrows before the Lord confident that He will answer me.

Day 20:

'And behold, there was a woman who had a spirit of infirmity eighteen years, and was bent over and could in no way raise herself up. But when Jesus saw her, He called her to Him and said to her, "Woman, you are loosed from your infirmity"

Luke 13:11-12 (NKJV)

The word 'infirmity' means to have a physical weakness, ailment or lack of strength. The passage here tells us that a woman had the spirit of infirmity for eighteen years. This is a significant period of time to be bound by something which keeps you in a weak state. But the good news is that when we trust and believe in God to release us from our past troubles, He will move on our behalf.

Don't be deceived into thinking that you have had your 'weakness' for too long. God can release you from whatever is gripping you despite how long it may have had reign in your life. The word says you are loosed! Believe it and claim your victory.

Affirmation: I believe, in Jesus name, that I am released from the things that weaken me.

Day 21:

'Repay no one evil for evil, but take thought for what is honest and proper and noble [aiming to be above reproach] in the sight of everyone'

Romans 12:17 (NKJV)

There are times in life when we will be hurt, insulted or indeed offended by others. At the extreme level we can also be betrayed by family, friends or acquaintances. If we are honest with ourselves we are also capable of causing other people to feel the same things.

Grudges can cause us to be bound by pain, hurt and resentment and can even lead to making us ill. But we do have a choice as to how we respond to being mistreated. Read the story of Joseph (Genesis 37-42) and see how he maintains a healthy positive attitude despite his trials and tribulations.

Even when others create negative environments for us or say hurtful things it should not be our desire to repay them for what they have done. We are encouraged by the Word to focus on doing good and being kind to others.

Affirmation: God is my defender so I can focus on being the best person I can be.

'He set my feet upon a rock, and established my steps. He has put a new song in my mouth – Praise to our God'

Psalm 40:1-2 (NKJV)

In times of trouble and adversity we have the opportunity to draw closer to God and build our faith. David is telling us here that when he waited upon the Lord, He heard his cry and then He moved on his behalf. He picked him up and then set his feet upon a rock. He made sure that David was placed on solid ground. But God does not do things in half measures because on top of rescuing him and steadying his ground, He establishes his steps and puts a new song in his mouth.

God will do the same for you. Regardless of the 'miry pit' that you may feel you are in God will take you out, steady your feet, establish your steps and give you a fresh portion of joy!

Affirmation: I will wait patiently upon the Lord.

'But David strengthened himself in the Lord his God'

1 Samuel 30:6 (NKJV)

Who or what do you rely on for your strength in times when you are feeling weak?

David faced many trials in his life and on every occasion he sought God and strengthened himself in this way. He called upon God in prayer. He was not prepared to act on his own wisdom and God consistently acted on his behalf.

Trust in the Lord and lean not on your own understanding. God knows and He is ready to act on our behalf. One of the ways of strengthening yourself is to speak the words of the Bible. Confess the scriptures that relate to the breakthroughs you need in your life.

Affirmation: I will strengthen myself in the Lord for I know He can and will act on my behalf.

'Village life ceased, it ceased in Israel. Until I, Deborah, arose, Arose a mother in Israel'

Judges 5:7 (NKJV)

Do not underestimate your value and your power as a woman. Deborah (in the Bible) is an epic story which sheds light on a mighty woman of God. She was wise, talented, respected and people sought her for her advice. She provided solutions to all who asked. When the situation arose that men became immobilised in a frightening situation it was Deborah who created the shift. Barak would not go to battle without her. He didn't feel that victory was achievable without her there.

When Deborah arose ('arose a mother in Israel') she changed the course of history for a group of people. Just like Deborah you have been blessed to change situations.

Affirmation: Just like Deborah I am able to make wise and Godly decisions.

Day 25:

'Yet who knows whether you have come to the kingdom for such a time as this?'

Esther 4:14 (NKJV)

When Esther entered into the palace she had no understanding
of just how important and significant that moment was. She was
on her way to fulfilling her destiny but had no clue. Sometimes I
believe that if God was to show us all of the plans He has for us we
would either run off or faint under the weight of it. So He reveals
section by section, knowing what we can handle.

Trust Him that His timing and His plans for you mean you are in the
right place. You have been born at the right time to the right parents
and God with your permission can complete what His word has set
out to do in your life. Learn to bloom where you are planted.

Affirmation: I will press on knowing that God has a plan for me.

'Now there was one, Anna, a prophetess, (....) and
this woman was a widow of eighty-four years who
did not depart from the temple, but served God with
fastings and prayers night and day'

Luke 2:37 (NKJV)

I think that Anna got the revelation that being in the temple was the
best place that she could possibly be. She knew that her blessing
and her very life force was contained in her relationship with God.
Now we do not have to be 'in the temple' day and night but we can
serve Him with our prayers, praise and worship.

In the morning we can offer a sacrifice of praise by getting up even
ten minutes earlier and reading our Bibles. We can put aside ten
minutes of our lunchbreak to pray. We can worship God in the car
by singing along to gospel music. Then at the end of the day we
can write a journal and testify of His goodness. We can pray and
intercede for others. We can be just like Anna and serve God night
and day.

**Affirmation: I want to deepen my relationship with you and I will
be consistent in my serving.**

'And He looked up and saw the rich putting their gifts into the treasury and He saw also a certain poor widow putting in two mites'

Luke 21:1-2 (NKJV)

Your contribution, no matter how small, matters. It shows the state of your heart and your attitude to giving. If you only give when you have more than enough you are no better than the rich putting their gifts into the treasury. When we trust God to supply our needs we can confidently give what little we have and know that God will bless it. God can take our smallest portion and multiply it.

If He has to move money or resources through a hundred hands to get it to you, He will. You cannot ever out give God. The widow's mites were worth much more in God's eyes because she gave it with a willing heart even when she had very little to offer.

Affirmation: I trust God to provide for me and I know He is the God of multiplication.

'I am doing a great work, so that I cannot come down. Why should the work cease while I leave it and go down to you?'

Nehemiah 6:3 (NKJV)

Nehemiah had been given the job of rebuilding the walls of Jerusalem. Whilst there were many that joined him and helped to complete the task, there were others who were sent to distract him.

Nehemiah knew the importance of the work he had been given to do. He was confident that God was with him and would help him to complete the job. When people rise up against us and seek to distract us from the work we have been given to do, we must be like Nehemiah and refuse to go down to the environment they want us to be in. Remember God's work is all great work.

Affirmation: I will be confident of my place in God's plans.

'But thanks be to God, who gives us the victory through our Lord Jesus Christ'

1 Corinthians 15:57 (NKJV)

Right now your faith, your joy, your peace, your hope and victory is returning to you. It is your portion and the Word declares that we have victory through our Lord. What awesome news! We have something to celebrate today (and every day) because God has assured us of this.

So, my dear sister, do not be down-hearted, do not continue to cry, do not be fearful but rejoice in the knowledge of this promise. When the Lord speaks we should listen. For in His words are promises untold and they have the ability to change your life. His words are prophetic and will lift burdens and cause yokes to be broken.

Affirmation: I win! I win! I win! In every situation I win for God's word has assured me of this.

Day 30:

'And you shall remember the Lord your God; for it is He who gives you power to get wealth, that He may establish His covenant which He swore to your fathers, as it is this day'

Deuteronomy 8:18 (NKJV)

There are seasons in your life when things are going well for you. You feel blessed and prosperity abounds in all areas of your life. You have the job you want and enjoy going to work. Your hobby has developed into a lucrative business idea. Your relationship is thriving and you feel secure. There is money in the bank and you have a choice of opportunities. It is at times like this (because of our selfish nature) that we tend to forget God and what He has done for us.

This word is a reminder of who has blessed us and who gives us the power to become wealthy. He promised to our spiritual forefathers that they would be blessed and He will establish the future generations of them. You are part of that generation.

Affirmation: I give honour and glory to my creator who provides for me in every area of my life.

'Who is wise and understanding among you? Let him show by good conduct that his works are done in the meekness of wisdom'

James 3:13 (NKJV)

You will have opportunities today to help someone else. You may get more than one chance to show your kindness and the love of Christ within you. I have a question for you – Is it easier to help someone when you know you will be rewarded for it? Another question – Who are you when no one is looking? Think of the story of the Good Samaritan (Luke 10:25-37).

You should strive to be wise in your kind deeds and not be seeking recognition as your motive for doing them. God will reward you even for what you do in secret to help someone.

Affirmation: Lord, I seek your wisdom and may my ways always be pleasing to you.

'The Lord who has been mindful of us will bless us'

Psalm 115:12 (NKJV)

God only wants good... No! Actually I correct myself – He only wants GREAT things for you. Even when our focus strays from Him, He waits patiently for you to return. He is 'mindful' (attentive or aware) of your life. He watches out for you because you are one of His precious daughters. There is a promise here; an assurance that He will (and not maybe) but definitely, bless you.

Maybe it's hard sometimes to believe this, especially if we judge God by man's standards. People may have promised things to you before and let you down but God's word stands. His word is steadfast. Get the revelation today and run with it – He will bless you.

Affirmation: I am confident that I will be blessed by Him.

Day 33:

'For who hath despised the day of small things?'

Zechariah 4:10 (NKJV)

Everyone who is now an expert was once a beginner.

There are global companies that exist now that were started in the kitchen or bedroom of humble homes. There are women who have been abused, rejected and poverty-stricken who have risen to great heights in their careers and personal lives.

Do not fear or become anxious about the humbleness or smallness of your beginnings. There is no need to accept the world's version of the story they have already written for you. God is the author of your life (if you will let him be) and He will take the small things and make them a training ground for your greatness. David, before he was a king, was the youngest and smallest in a large family. He tended sheep and yet He and not his brothers killed Goliath.

Affirmation: I will take the time to learn the lessons needed from my humble beginnings.

Day 34:

'The spirit of God has made me, and the breath of the Almighty gives me life'

Job 33:4 (NKJV)

We all live in a busy world with many competing deadlines and matters we have to attend to. Often as women we take on many things and risk getting burnt out and feeling tired and fed up. It is easy in such an environment to forget who we are and where we should draw our strength from on a daily basis.

This word from the book of Job (a man who was severely tested with trials and tribulations) reminds us of who made us and how we came to have life. It is good to be confident of who it is that has given you life. Our Lord who is our creator has breathed life into us and caused us to be here.

Affirmation: I declare that I have been formed by a mighty Father and creator.

'Arise, shine; for your light has come! And the glory of the Lord is risen upon you'

Isaiah 60:1 (NKJV)

A new season beckons. You can arise and allow your talents, skills and abilities to shine. As women we often underplay our achievements and humbly deny that our successes are worth really celebrating. This is false humility and we should not fall into the trap of behaving in this manner. God has given you the talent to do certain things and has placed His light within you.

Have you ever thought that when you hide your talents or undervalue your abilities you may be subconsciously causing someone else to hide also? You may not help whom you have been created to help or attract others to the Kingdom of God because you do not allow your light to shine.

Affirmation: I have a light placed within me and I will allow it to shine each and every day.

Day 36:

'Then all your people will be righteous and they will possess the land forever. They are the shoot I have planted, the work of my hands, for the display of my splendour'

Isaiah 60:21 (NIV)

Do you ever question your beauty or attractiveness? Do you compare yourself against your family, friends and colleagues? If asked the question today, how do you feel about you? I wonder how positive your answer would be. I can imagine that like everyone else that answer can fluctuate from day to day.

God has bestowed (placed) His beauty upon you. That is a given word and it means that our answer doesn't have to be related to our circumstances, our hairstyle, our weight, our ethnicity or our status. You have perfect beauty because it has been made perfect through His splendour.

Affirmation: My beauty was created by God and I delight in it.

Day 37:

'Before I formed you in the womb I knew you. Before you were born I sanctified you'

Jeremiah 1:5 (NKJV)

God was thinking about you and in fact knew you even before He created you. Wow! What an awesome fact. This tells me and it should encourage you that He must have an amazing plan for your life. Why would He sanctify you even before you were born? If you were not destined to be someone special and have great purpose about you then why would He have spent such time and energy on you?

You have been blessed even before you were created. This means that it doesn't matter about the circumstances of your birth (in the natural) or indeed the state of your birth parents. God has a special plan for you because He has sanctified you and named you special.

Affirmation: I offer my praises to you Lord for you have sanctified me.

'The spirit you have received is not a spirit of slavery, leading back into a life of fear, but a spirit of adoption, enabling you to cry 'Abba Father'

Romans 8:15 (Revised English Bible)

There are people and indeed situations that can enter our lives that cause anxiety and fear to rise within us. You may not be in physical slavery but can still be very much oppressed by mental slavery; your thoughts held captive by things that overwhelm you, degrade you and ultimately can destroy you. The good news from the gospel declares that we have been adopted into the family of God and therefore we can confidently call upon Him.

We do not have to be afraid any longer or wrestle to be free from a spirit of slavery. Call to Him 'Abba Father' and He will answer you in His perfect timing.

Affirmation: I have a spirit of boldness because I know who my Father is.

'And Joshua the son of Nun sent out of Shittim two men to spy secretly, saying, Go view the land, even Jericho. And they went, and came into an harlot's house, named Rahab, and lodged there'

Joshua 1:1-2 (NKJV)

When we first meet Rahab she is named as a prostitute. Even in today's society that word holds negative imagery and a person named as such would not be very well respected. Rahab had an opportunity to help the spies sent by Joshua, and in so doing assisted in the plan of God. She was obedient and did all she could to help the spies escape.

God could have chosen anyone to help but he sought out whom most others would have disregarded. God genuinely desires to connect with the lost, the prostitutes, the drug users, the criminals and anyone who believes all hope has gone. Do not ever believe you have gone so far wrong that God cannot save you and use you as part of His plan.

God rewards obedience – In Matthew 1:5 Rahab is named in the genealogy of Jesus Christ as the mother of Boaz. He transforms her from harlot to heroine and prostitute to proud wife and mother.

Affirmation: My mistakes can all be put behind me because I put my life in His hands.

Day 40:

'Be obedient to God your Father, and do not let your characters be shaped any longer by the desires you cherished in your days of ignorance'

1 Peter 1:14 (Revised English Bible)

Every one of us has a past. Some of it will have been positive and productive and some of it less so. God wants us to step boldly into our position of royalty that He declared for us even before we were born. You have to believe in your heart and confess with your mouth that you only want to go forward and get closer and closer to God.

Put behind you the desires that you held in your days of ignorance because you know better now. Ask God to continue to enlighten you, to strengthen you in His understanding and to let His love be your comfort.

Affirmation: My past is behind me and my latter days will be greater than my former days.

<u>Last Thoughts</u>

I pray that you have been blessed by this book and the words within. If you live in Croydon, Surrey or the surrounding areas or are ever visiting please accept this invitation to come and visit Rhema Church London (www.rhema.co.uk). We meet every Sunday at 11am at the Fairfield Halls in Croydon.

If you have not accepted Jesus as your Lord and Saviour please take a minute to say this prayer:

"Heavenly Father, have mercy on me, a sinner. I believe in you and that your word is true. I believe that Jesus Christ is the Son of the living God and that he died on the cross so that I may now have forgiveness for my sins and eternal life. I know that without you in my heart my life is meaningless.

I believe in my heart that You, Father God, raised Jesus from the dead. Please, Father, forgive me for every sin I have ever committed or done in my heart. Jesus, please come into my heart as my personal Lord, Saviour and friend today.

I give you my life and ask you to take full control from this moment on; I pray this in the name of Jesus Christ."

Amen.